MY MUSCLE BUILDER BOOK 2
Piano Technique for Young Beginners

Jennifer Boster, NCTM
theplayfulpiano.com

Copyright ©2023 Jennifer Boster
The Playful Piano | theplayfulpiano.com

All rights reserved. No part of this publication may be reproduced or transmitted in any form or by any means without written permission from the author.

The Playful Piano
PO Box 12931
Ogden, UT 84412-2931
USA

This book belongs to:

_____

My piano teacher is:

_____

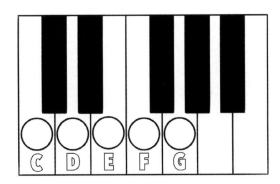

Note to Piano Teachers

Welcome to My Muscle Builder Books!

My Muscle Builder Books are illustrated step-by-step piano technique books designed to help even your youngest students become fluent in playing chords and scales all over the keyboard. Too often our students get stuck in C position and G position, and it takes too long to venture out into other keys and areas of the keyboard.

Once your students complete this book, they will be more confident playing the seven white-key major chords, pentascales and arpeggios, and they will also learn how to change these to minor. They will learn how to invert chords, how to transpose a simple melody to a different key, and they will get lots of practice playing their scales, arpeggios and chords in several different ways.

Because this series is designed to be used right from the very first lesson, scales and chords are not notated on the staff. Instead, the scales are shown using illustrations.

This new edition of the popular My Muscle Builder Book series is in the format of a coloring book! This not only makes it easier and more cost-effective to print copies of the studio-licensed version and to produce paperback copies, but it gives students a fun way to track their practicing and encourages them to play each scale multiple times throughout the week. Each page of exercises has something to color to help track the number of times they have practiced each exercise.

These books were designed to be used alongside your method book or piano pieces of choice. As students consistently progress through all of the levels of the My Muscle Builder Books, they will learn good piano technique, learn chords and scales in every key on the piano, and will have a solid foundation for learning more advanced scales and arpeggios. They will be ready to play with confidence when new chords and keys are introduced in their method books and repertoire.

I hope you enjoy these books!

-Jenny Boster, NCTM

MAJOR CHORDS SPELLING BEE

Chords are made up of skips. Understanding the notes that make up each chord can help you understand music theory, so it is important to be able to spell each chord.

Practice saying the musical alphabet in skips to get ready to spell chords. Try starting on different letters:

"A-C-E-G-B-D-F"
"G-B-D-F-A-C-E"
"D-F-A-C-E-G-B"

MAJOR CHORDS SPELLING BEE

Spell a C Major Chord
____ ____ ____

Color a C Major Chord:

Spell a D Major Chord
____ ____ ____

Color a D Major Chord:

Spell an E Major Chord
____ ____ ____

Color an E Major Chord:

Spell an F Major Chord
____ ____ ____

Color an F Major Chord:

Spell a G Major Chord
____ ____ ____

Color a G Major Chord:

Spell an A Major Chord
____ ____ ____

Color an A Major Chord:

Spell a B Major Chord
____ ____ ____

Color a B Major Chord:

MAJOR AND MINOR

Different types of scales have different sound qualities. So far we have learned **major** scales and chords. Now we will learn to play **minor** scales and chords. Have your teacher play you some major and minor scales chords so you can hear the difference.

What do major and minor sound like to you? How would you describe the sound?

Major sounds like: _____

Minor sounds like: _____

HOW TO PLAY A MINOR 5-FINGER SCALE:

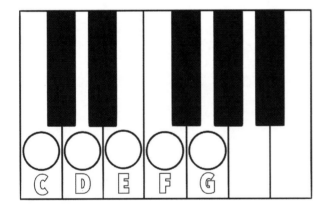

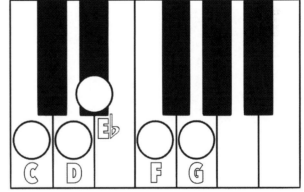

First play a **major** 5-finger scale...

Then lower the **third note** one half step, or to the very next note to the left. That's it! Let's practice changing all of the major scales we have learned to minor scales.

7

C MAJOR C MINOR

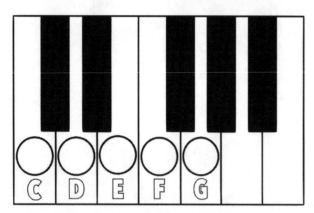 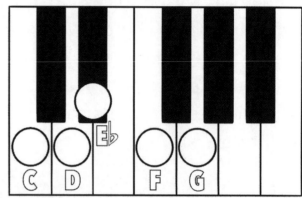

- Play a C major scale hands together; sing **"Tip-toe up the keys"** and **"Tip-toe down the keys"**

- Now play a C major **chord** – which 3 notes are part of the chord? Color those 3 notes.

- Play a C **minor** scale hands together; sing **"Tip-toe up the keys"** and **"Tip-toe down the keys."** Remember to change the middle note one half step lower.

- Now play a **C minor chord** – which 3 notes are part of the chord? Color those 3 notes.

Color a cat every time you practice this page!

REMEMBER:
Cupcake Hands (not Pancake Hands!), Firm Fingertips, Flexible Wrist

G MAJOR G MINOR

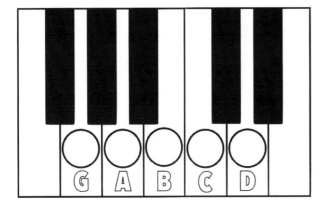 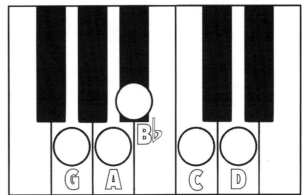

- Play a G major scale hands together; sing **"Tip-toe up the keys"** and **"Tip-toe down the keys"**

- Now play a G major **chord** – which 3 notes are part of the chord? Color those 3 notes.

- Play a G **minor** scale hands together; sing **"Tip-toe up the keys"** and **"Tip-toe down the keys."** Remember to change the middle note one half step lower.

- Now play a **G minor chord** – which 3 notes are part of the chord? Color those 3 notes.

Color a goat every time you practice this page!

REMEMBER:
Cupcake Hands (not Pancake Hands!), Firm Fingertips, Flexible Wrist

F MAJOR   F MINOR

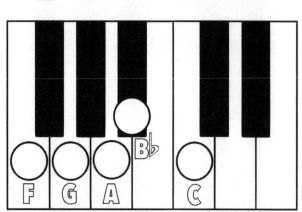
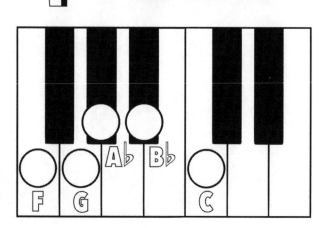

- Play an F major scale hands together; sing **"Tip-toe up the keys"** and **"Tip-toe down the keys"**

- Now play an F major **chord** – which 3 notes are part of the chord? Color those 3 notes.

- Play an F **minor** scale hands together; sing **"Tip-toe up the keys"** and **"Tip-toe down the keys."** Remember to change the middle note one half step lower.

- Now play an **F minor chord** – which 3 notes are part of the chord? Color those 3 notes.

Color a flamingo every time you practice this page!

REMEMBER:
Cupcake Hands
(not Pancake Hands!),
Firm Fingertips,
Flexible Wrist

D MAJOR  # D MINOR

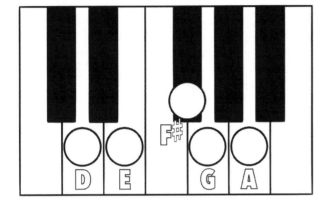 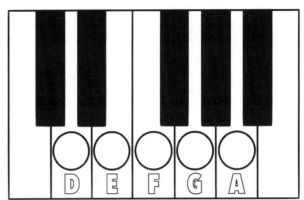

- Play a D major scale hands together; sing **"Tip-toe up the keys"** and **"Tip-toe down the keys"**

- Now play a D major **chord** – which 3 notes are part of the chord? Color those 3 notes.

- Play a D **minor** scale hands together; sing **"Tip-toe up the keys"** and **"Tip-toe down the keys."** Remember to change the middle note one half step lower.

- Now play a **D minor chord** – which 3 notes are part of the chord? Color those 3 notes.

Color a dog every time you practice this page!

REMEMBER:
Cupcake Hands (not Pancake Hands!), Firm Fingertips, Flexible Wrist

A MAJOR  # A MINOR

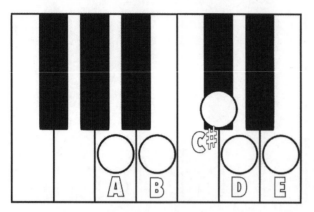 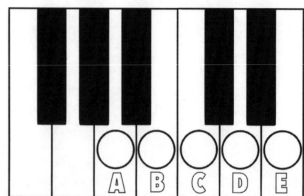

- Play an A major scale hands together; sing **"Tip-toe up the keys"** and **"Tip-toe down the keys"**

- Now play an A major **chord** – which 3 notes are part of the chord? Color those 3 notes.

- Play an A **minor** scale hands together; sing **"Tip-toe up the keys"** and **"Tip-toe down the keys."** Remember to change the middle note one half step lower.

- Now play an **A minor chord** – which 3 notes are part of the chord? Color those 3 notes.

Color an alligator every time you practice this page!

REMEMBER:
Cupcake Hands
(not Pancake Hands!),
Firm Fingertips,
Flexible Wrist

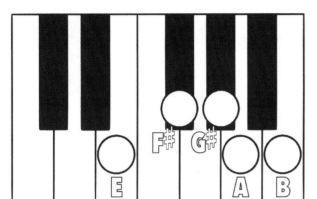 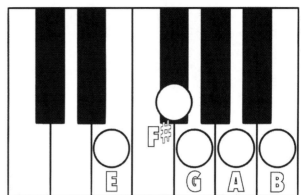

- Play an E major scale hands together; sing **"Tip-toe up the keys"** and **"Tip-toe down the keys"**

- Now play an E major **chord** – which 3 notes are part of the chord? Color those 3 notes.

- Play an E **minor** scale hands together; sing **"Tip-toe up the keys"** and **"Tip-toe down the keys."** Remember to change the middle note one half step lower.

- Now play an **E minor chord** – which 3 notes are part of the chord? Color those 3 notes.

Color an elephant every time you practice this page!

REMEMBER:
Cupcake Hands
(not Pancake Hands!),
Firm Fingertips,
Flexible Wrist

13

B MAJOR   # B MINOR

- Play a B major scale hands together; sing **"Tip-toe up the keys"** and **"Tip-toe down the keys"**

- Now play a B major **chord** – which 3 notes are part of the chord? Color those 3 notes.

- Play a B **minor** scale hands together; sing **"Tip-toe up the keys"** and **"Tip-toe down the keys."** Remember to change the middle note one half step lower.

- Now play a **B minor chord** – which 3 notes are part of the chord? Color those 3 notes.

Color a bear every time you practice this page!

REMEMBER:
Cupcake Hands (not Pancake Hands!), Firm Fingertips, Flexible Wrist

FANCY ARPEGGIOS

Imagine you are on a big stage at a beautiful grand piano, with an audience watching you practice your arpeggios! You are wearing a fancy outfit and the spotlight is on you. Can you play your arpeggios extra **fancy** and **musical** today? Here are the rules:

- Sit up straight
- No scooting up the bench - sit in the middle and lean to the left or right
- Hold down the damper (right) pedal the entire time
- Curve those fingers
- Make it musical & beautiful
- Keep it steady and flowing - **no pausing between arpeggios!**

FANCY ARPEGGIOS: C MAJOR

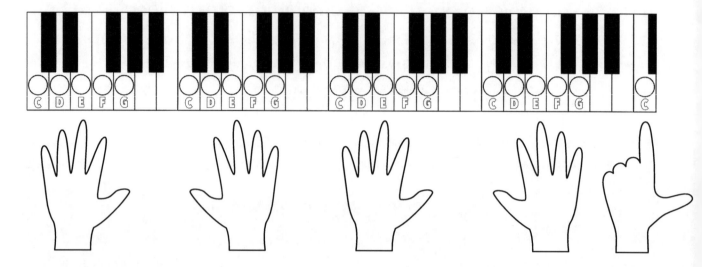

- Find and **color** all of the notes in a C major arpeggio
- Play a **four-octave, hand-over-hand fancy arpeggio!** Start with your left hand as shown above. When you reach the top, play a high C with your left hand, then come back down and end back at the bottom with your left hand

WAYS TO MAKE IT MORE FANCY

- Start quiet, then get louder as the notes go higher! Get softer as the notes get lower again.
- Use firm fingertips to play with a beautiful tone. Be confident!
- Try it with the metronome to keep it steady

REMEMBER:
Sit up straight
Sit in center of bench, no scooting!
Hold down the pedal
Curve those fingers
Keep it steady: no pausing
Make it musical!

Color a cupcake every time you practice this page!

FANCY ARPEGGIOS: G MAJOR

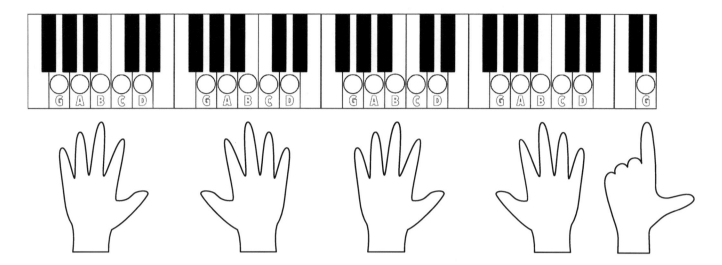

- Find and **color** all of the notes in a G major arpeggio
- Play a **four-octave, hand-over-hand fancy arpeggio!** Start with your left hand as shown above. When you reach the top, play a high G with your left hand, then come back down and end back at the bottom with your left hand

WAYS TO MAKE IT MORE FANCY

- Start quiet, then get louder as the notes go higher! Get softer as the notes get lower again.
- Use firm fingertips to play with a beautiful tone. Be confident!
- Try it with the metronome to keep it steady

Color a giraffe every time you practice this page!

REMEMBER:
Sit up straight
Sit in center of bench, no scooting!
Hold down the pedal
Curve those fingers
Keep it steady: no pausing
Make it musical!

FANCY ARPEGGIOS: F MAJOR

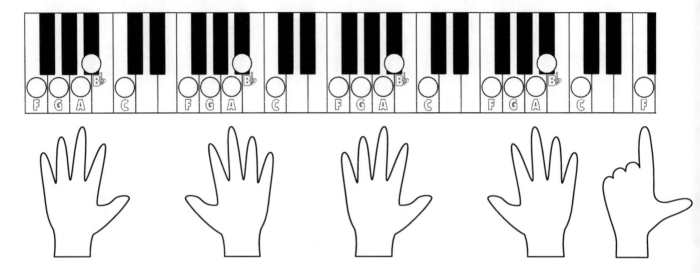

- Find and **color** all of the notes in a F major arpeggio
- Play a **four-octave, hand-over-hand fancy arpeggio!** Start with your left hand as shown above. When you reach the top, play a high F with your left hand, then come back down and end back at the bottom with your left hand

WAYS TO MAKE IT MORE FANCY

- Start quiet, then get louder as the notes go higher! Get softer as the notes get lower again.
- Use firm fingertips to play with a beautiful tone. Be confident!
- Try it with the metronome to keep it steady

Color a pair of flip-flops every time you practice this page!

REMEMBER:
Sit up straight
Sit in center of bench, no scooting!
Hold down the pedal
Curve those fingers
Keep it steady: no pausing
Make it musical!

FANCY ARPEGGIOS: D MAJOR

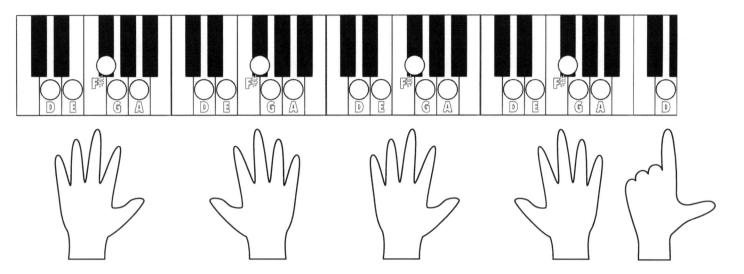

- Find and **color** all of the notes in a D major arpeggio
- Play a **four-octave, hand-over-hand fancy arpeggio!** Start with your left hand as shown above. When you reach the top, play a high D with your left hand, then come back down and end back at the bottom with your left hand

WAYS TO MAKE IT MORE FANCY

- Start quiet, then get louder as the notes go higher! Get softer as the notes get lower again.
- Use firm fingertips to play with a beautiful tone. Be confident!
- Try it with the metronome to keep it steady

REMEMBER:
Sit up straight
Sit in center of bench, no scooting!
Hold down the pedal
Curve those fingers
Keep it steady: no pausing
Make it musical!

Color a donut every time you practice this page!

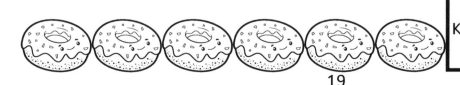

FANCY ARPEGGIOS: A MAJOR

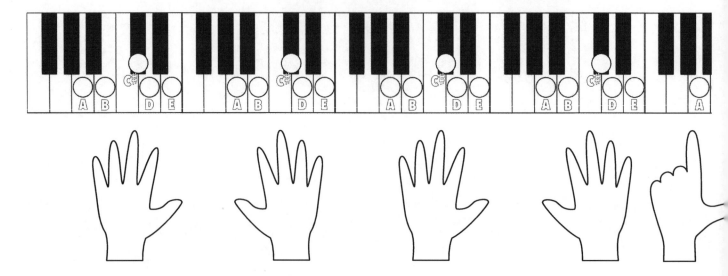

- Find and **color** all of the notes in an A major arpeggio
- Play a **four-octave, hand-over-hand fancy arpeggio!** Start with your left hand as shown above. When you reach the top, play a high A with your left hand, then come back down and end back at the bottom with your left hand

WAYS TO MAKE IT MORE FANCY

- Start quiet, then get louder as the notes go higher! Get softer as the notes get lower again.
- Use firm fingertips to play with a beautiful tone. Be confident!
- Try it with the metronome to keep it steady

Color an astronaut every time you practice this page!

REMEMBER:
Sit up straight
Sit in center of bench, no scooting!
Hold down the pedal
Curve those fingers
Keep it steady: no pausing
Make it musical!

FANCY ARPEGGIOS: E MAJOR

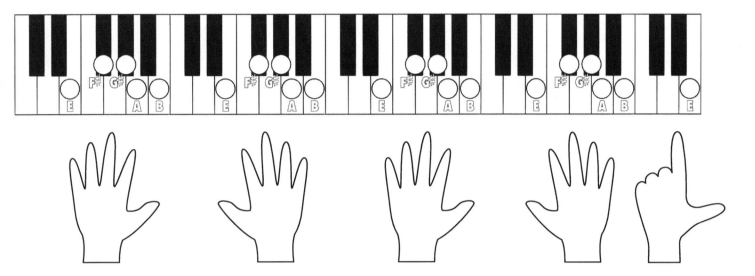

- Find and **color** all of the notes in an E major arpeggio
- Play a **four-octave, hand-over-hand fancy arpeggio!** Start with your left hand as shown above. When you reach the top, play a high E with your left hand, then come back down and end back at the bottom with your left hand

WAYS TO MAKE IT MORE FANCY

- Start quiet, then get louder as the notes go higher! Get softer as the notes get lower again.
- Use firm fingertips to play with a beautiful tone. Be confident!
- Try it with the metronome to keep it steady

Color an eel every time you practice this page!

REMEMBER:
Sit up straight
Sit in center of bench, no scooting!
Hold down the pedal
Curve those fingers
Keep it steady: no pausing
Make it musical!

FANCY ARPEGGIOS: B MAJOR

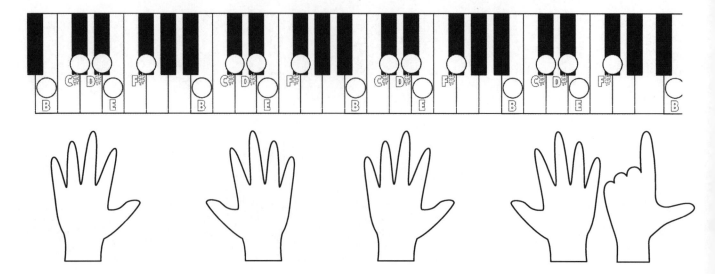

- Find and **color** all of the notes in a B major arpeggio
- Play a **four-octave, hand-over-hand fancy arpeggio!** Start with your left hand as shown above. When you reach the top, play a high B with your left hand, then come back down and end back at the bottom with your left hand

WAYS TO MAKE IT MORE FANCY

- Start quiet, then get louder as the notes go higher! Get softer as the notes get lower again.
- Use firm fingertips to play with a beautiful tone. Be confident!
- Try it with the metronome to keep it steady

Color a bumblebee every time you practice this page!

REMEMBER:
Sit up straight
Sit in center of bench, no scooting!
Hold down the pedal
Curve those fingers
Keep it steady: no pausing
Make it musical!

STACCATO SCALES

Can you play your scales STACCATO - short, detached and bouncy? Remember to keep your fingers curved, and to BOUNCE your fingertips off of the keys like a bouncy ball!

C MAJOR
○○○○○○○○ Right hand alone
○○○○○○○○ Left hand alone
○○○○○○○○ Hands together

G MAJOR
○○○○○○○○ Right hand alone
○○○○○○○○ Left hand alone
○○○○○○○○ Hands together

D MAJOR
○○○○○○○○ Right hand alone
○○○○○○○○ Left hand alone
○○○○○○○○ Hands together

A MAJOR
○○○○○○○○ Right hand alone
○○○○○○○○ Left hand alone
○○○○○○○○ Hands together

E MAJOR
○○○○○○○○ Right hand alone
○○○○○○○○ Left hand alone
○○○○○○○○ Hands together

B MAJOR
○○○○○○○○ Right hand alone
○○○○○○○○ Left hand alone
○○○○○○○○ Hands together

F MAJOR
○○○○○○○○ Right hand alone
○○○○○○○○ Left hand alone
○○○○○○○○ Hands together

LEGATO SCALES

Now let's play our scales LEGATO - smooth and connected! Make sure there is *no space in-between notes.* Remember to keep your fingers curved! Drop your wrist down on the first note, then lift up gracefully on the last note to make a nice musical phrase.

C MAJOR
○○○○○○○○ Right hand alone
○○○○○○○○ Left hand alone
○○○○○○○○ Hands together

G MAJOR
○○○○○○○○ Right hand alone
○○○○○○○○ Left hand alone
○○○○○○○○ Hands together

D MAJOR
○○○○○○○○ Right hand alone
○○○○○○○○ Left hand alone
○○○○○○○○ Hands together

A MAJOR
○○○○○○○○ Right hand alone
○○○○○○○○ Left hand alone
○○○○○○○○ Hands together

E MAJOR
○○○○○○○○ Right hand alone
○○○○○○○○ Left hand alone
○○○○○○○○ Hands together

B MAJOR
○○○○○○○○ Right hand alone
○○○○○○○○ Left hand alone
○○○○○○○○ Hands together

F MAJOR
○○○○○○○○ Right hand alone
○○○○○○○○ Left hand alone
○○○○○○○○ Hands together

TRANSPOSING

You are getting so good at these scales! Using your scales knowledge, you can now change, or **transpose**, a song from one key into another! Your teacher will help you pick some simple five-finger pieces that you can transpose into other keys. Color a butterfly once you transpose to a key three times!

C MAJOR
Color in the five notes of the C major 5-finger scale: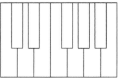
 Transpose 3 short pieces to this key

G MAJOR
Color in the five notes of the G major 5-finger scale: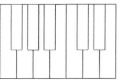
 Transpose 3 short pieces to this key

F MAJOR
Color in the five notes of the F major 5-finger scale: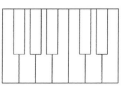
 Transpose 3 short pieces to this key

REMEMBER:
Find the five-finger hand position & stay there. Watch carefully for steps & skips.

TRANSPOSING

D MAJOR — Color in the five notes of the D major 5-finger scale:
Transpose 3 short pieces to this key

A MAJOR — Color in the five notes of the A major 5-finger scale:
Transpose 3 short pieces to this key

E MAJOR — Color in the five notes of the E major 5-finger scale:
Transpose 3 short pieces to this key

B MAJOR — Color in the five notes of the B major 5-finger scale:
Transpose 3 short pieces to this key

MAJOR & MINOR ARPEGGIOS & CHORDS

Can you play an arpeggio and a chord in EACH major and minor key we've learned so far? As you play sing "Ar-pe-ggio, Chord!" or count "1,2,3, 1-2-3!"

		MAJOR	MINOR
	Color the 3 arpeggio notes on each picture ☆ Play "ar-pe-ggio, chord" ☆☆☆☆ - first major, then minor	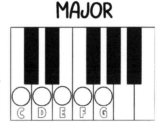	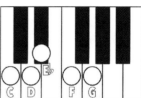
	Color the 3 arpeggio notes on each picture ☆ Play "ar-pe-ggio, chord" ☆☆☆☆ - first major, then minor	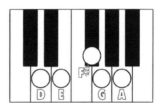	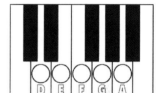
	Color the 3 arpeggio notes on each picture ☆ Play "ar-pe-ggio, chord" ☆☆☆☆ - first major, then minor		
	Color the 3 arpeggio notes on each picture ☆ Play "ar-pe-ggio, chord" ☆☆☆☆ - first major, then minor	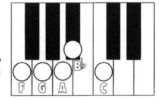	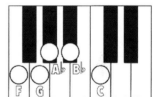
	Color the 3 arpeggio notes on each picture ☆ Play "ar-pe-ggio, chord" ☆☆☆☆ - first major, then minor		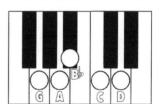
	Color the 3 arpeggio notes on each picture ☆ Play "ar-pe-ggio, chord" ☆☆☆☆ - first major, then minor	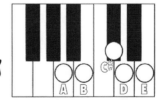	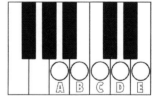
	Color the 3 arpeggio notes on each picture ☆ Play "ar-pe-ggio, chord" ☆☆☆☆ - first major, then minor	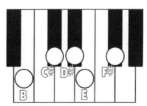	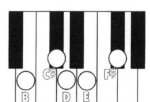

ARPEGGIOS & CHORDS CHALLENGE

CHALLENGE: Can you play all of the white key MAJOR AND MINOR arpeggios & chords right in a ROW? Play them just like you did on the previous page, but all 7 keys one right after the other like this:

C Major: "Ar-pe-ggio, Chord!"
C Minor: "Ar-pe-ggio, Chord!"

D Major: "Ar-pe-ggio, Chord!"
D Minor: "Ar-pe-ggio, Chord!"

E Major: "Ar-pe-ggio, Chord!"
E Minor: "Ar-pe-ggio, Chord!"

F Major: "Ar-pe-ggio, Chord!"
F Minor: "Ar-pe-ggio, Chord!"

G Major: "Ar-pe-ggio, Chord!"
G Minor: "Ar-pe-ggio, Chord!"

A Major: "Ar-pe-ggio, Chord!"
A Minor: "Ar-pe-ggio, Chord!"

B Major: "Ar-pe-ggio, Chord!"
B Minor: "Ar-pe-ggio, Chord!"

Color a star each time you play them all in a row:

OPPOSITE-MOTION SCALES

You know your scales so well, let's make it a little more fun and challenging! Play a **scale going up with your right hand** while you play a **scale going down with your left hand**!

TIP: Place both hands on the correct hand position, then start playing, starting on your thumbs. You will play going outward, then switch directions to come back inward, ending on your thumbs.

You can do it! Color or put a sticker in the circle each time you practice each scale.

○○○○○○○ C Major opposite-motion scale
○○○○○○○ D Major opposite-motion scale
○○○○○○○ E Major opposite-motion scale
○○○○○○○ F Major opposite-motion scale
○○○○○○○ G Major opposite-motion scale
○○○○○○○ A Major opposite-motion scale
○○○○○○○ B Major opposite-motion scale

CHORD INVERSIONS

Once you know how to spell a chord, you can switch the order of the notes and play it in lots of different positions all over the piano! You can play the notes in a C chord in any order on the piano, and it will still be a C chord! Let's try it:

First, let's review how to spell a C chord. Circle all of the notes you can find that are in a C major chord:

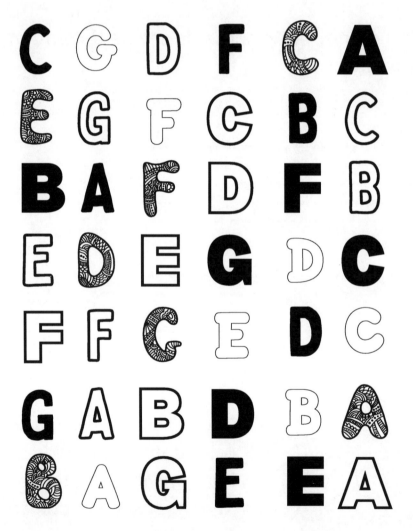

Now choose ANY C, ANY E, and ANY G on the piano and play it - that is a C chord! Maybe you choose a really low G, a middle C and a high E - that is a C chord! You could even play more than one of each note - get a friend to help you!

CHORD INVERSIONS

Chord inversions are chords that are played with the notes in a different order. First play the chord in "root position" - or the regular chord you already know.

To make a chord inversion, take the bottom note of the chord and **leap frog** that note over the whole chord to **play that note one octave higher**. So instead of playing C-E-G, now you'll play E-G-C! Next, leap frog that E up to the higher E, and you'll now play G-C-E. If you leap frog the bottom note one more time, you arrive back at root position.

Now you get to try it! We will do it with your **right hand only**. We will do it two ways - walking up the keys one at a time, and playing all three notes at once in chords. **Make sure you follow the fingering!**

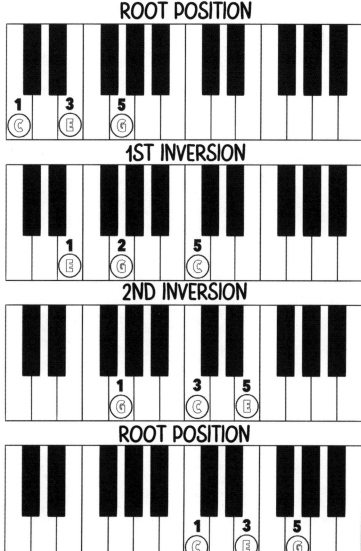

31

C MAJOR CHORD INVERSIONS

- Spell a C Major chord: _____ _____ _____

- Play the chord inversions by walking up the keys with your right hand, and name the letters as you go ☆☆☆☆☆

- Play the inversions in block chords ☆☆☆☆☆

REMEMBER:
It is very important to use the correct fingering!

ROOT POSITION
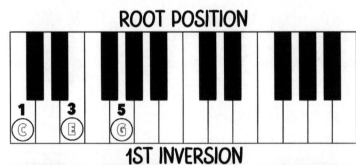

1ST INVERSION
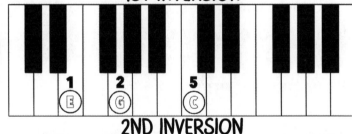

2ND INVERSION
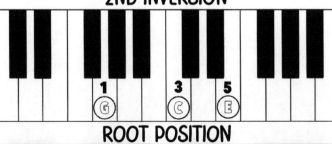

ROOT POSITION
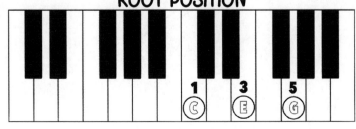

D MAJOR CHORD INVERSIONS

- Spell a D Major chord: ___ ___ ___

- Play the chord inversions by walking up the keys with your right hand, and name the letters as you go ☆☆☆☆☆

- Play the inversions in block chords ☆☆☆☆☆

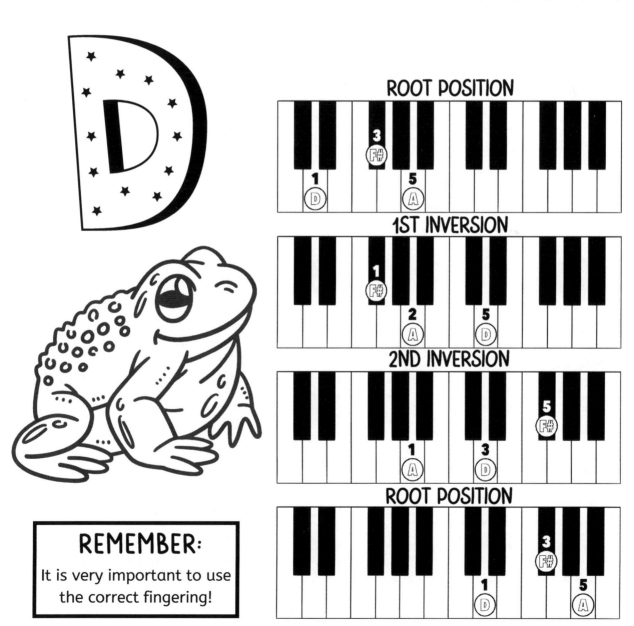

REMEMBER:
It is very important to use the correct fingering!

E MAJOR CHORD INVERSIONS

- Spell an E Major chord: _____ _____ _____

- Play the chord inversions by walking up the keys with your right hand, and name the letters as you go ☆☆☆☆☆☆

- Play the inversions in block chords ☆☆☆☆☆☆

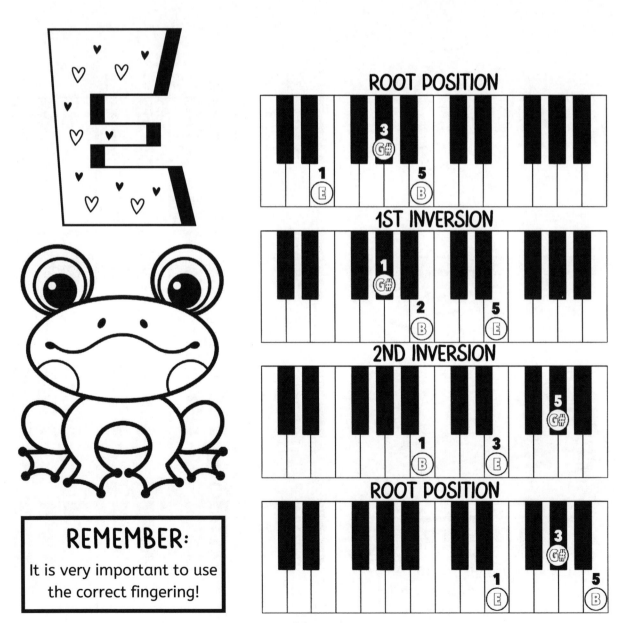

REMEMBER:
It is very important to use the correct fingering!

F MAJOR CHORD INVERSIONS

- Spell an F Major chord: ___ ___ ___

- Play the chord inversions by walking up the keys with your right hand, and name the letters as you go ☆☆☆☆☆☆

- Play the inversions in block chords ☆☆☆☆☆☆

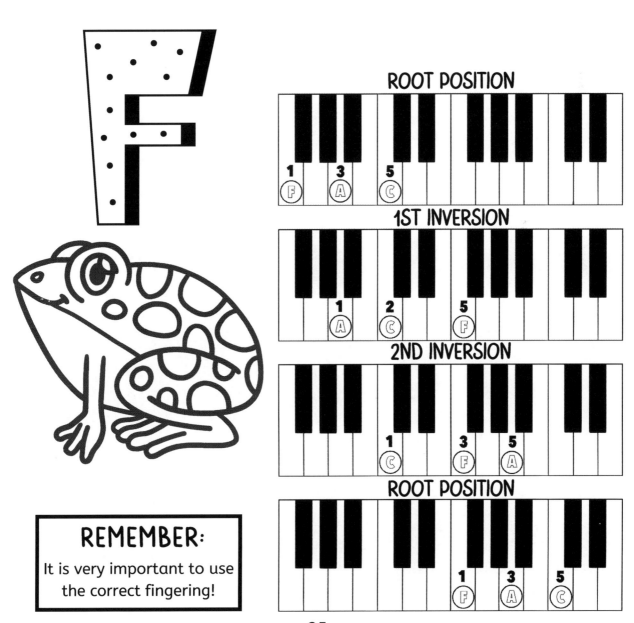

REMEMBER: It is very important to use the correct fingering!

35

G MAJOR CHORD INVERSIONS

- Spell a G Major chord: ____ ____ ____

- Play the chord inversions by walking up the keys with your right hand, and name the letters as you go ☆☆☆☆☆

- Play the inversions in block chords ☆☆☆☆☆

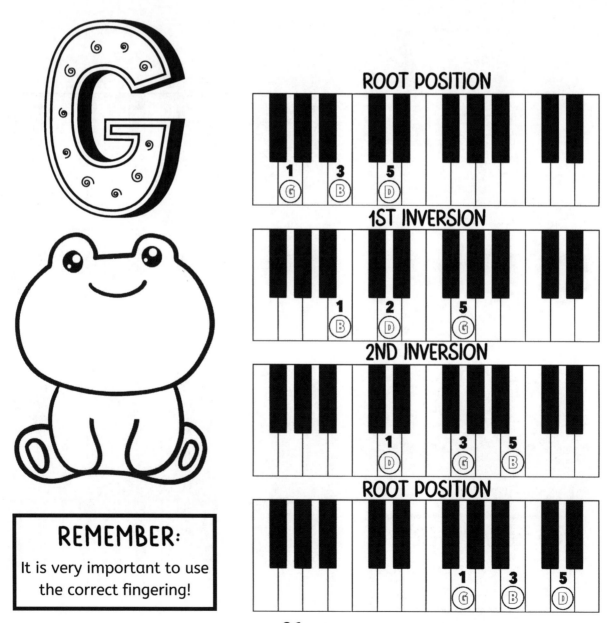

REMEMBER:
It is very important to use the correct fingering!

A MAJOR CHORD INVERSIONS

- Spell an A Major chord: ____ ____ ____

- Play the chord inversions by walking up the keys with your right hand, and name the letters as you go

- Play the inversions in block chords

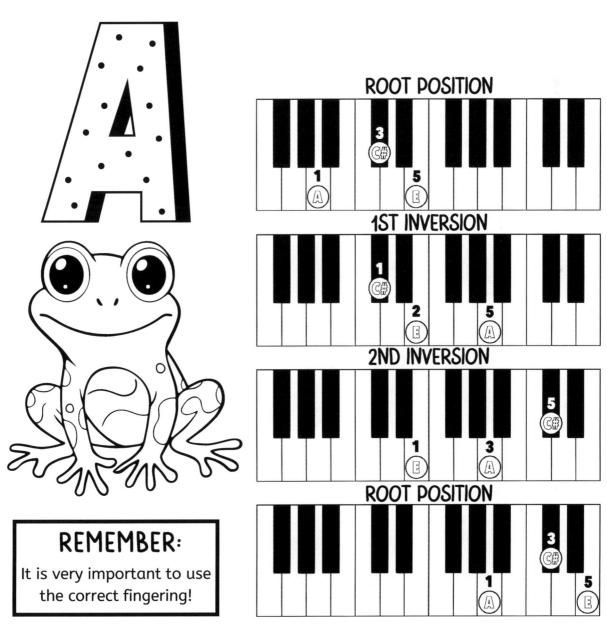

REMEMBER: It is very important to use the correct fingering!

B MAJOR CHORD INVERSIONS

- Spell a B Major chord: _____ _____ _____

- Play the chord inversions by walking up the keys with your right hand, and name the letters as you go

- Play the inversions in block chords

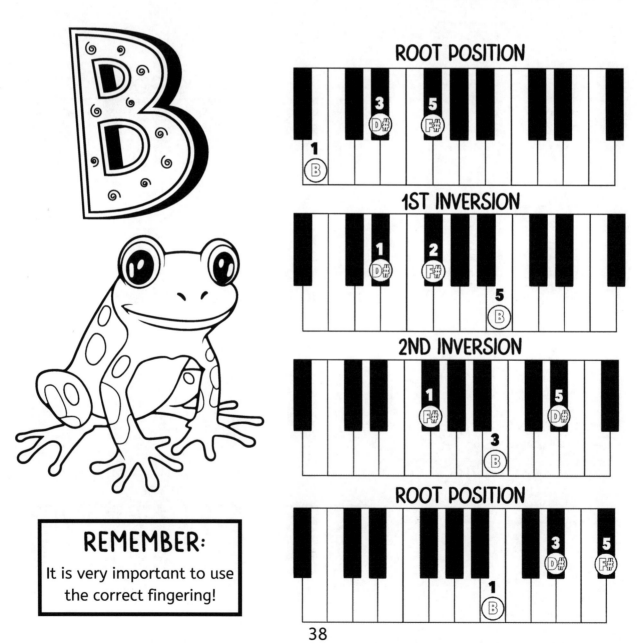

REMEMBER: It is very important to use the correct fingering!

WAY TO GO!
YOU FINISHED THE BOOK.

You are ready to move onto Book 3!

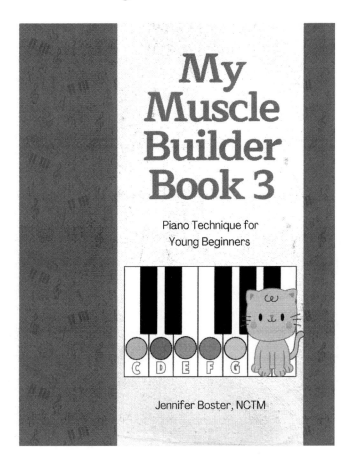

ABOUT THE AUTHOR

Jenny Boster has been playing the piano and creating things ever since she was a little girl. She loves combining her interests to create fun and original resources for piano teachers. She has loved teaching piano lessons for over twenty-five years. Jenny has a Bachelor of Music degree in Piano Performance from Brigham Young University and is a Nationally-Certified Teacher of Music. She frequently speaks at music teacher conferences and has become an advocate of female composers. Jenny is passionate about encouraging students to listen to and gain a love for classical music. Her greatest joys are her husband, Jonathan, and being a mother to her five children.

TECHNIQUE BOOKS FROM THE PLAYFUL PIANO

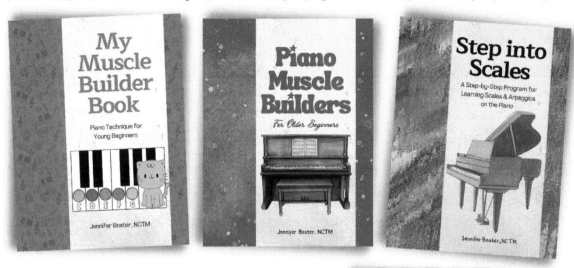

My Muscle Builder Book series

Brand new edition!! Books 1 and 2 available now, other books coming soon. Pentascales, simple arpeggios & chords for beginners. Use from the very first lesson to get your students comfortable playing chords and scales all over the piano!

Piano Muscle Builders for Older Beginners

All-in-one edition! Accelerated version of My Muscle Builder Books for older beginners. Learn pentascales, simple arpeggios and chords in all major and minor keys; learn inversions in 7 major and minor keys and chord progressions in 7 major keys.

Step Into Scales

COMPREHENSIVE SCALE BOOK created to follow the My Muscle Builder Book series or Piano Muscle Builders for Older Beginners. A step-by-step program for learning full scales & arpeggios. Learn 4-octave major & 3 types of minor scales, arpeggios, blocked and broken inversion exercises, basic chord progressions, Russian scales and 1-2 ratio contrary scales in all keys. Easy to implement and follow, motivating to complete and customizable order of teaching. Also includes thumb prep exercises and scale clusters to warm up and learn scale notes & fingerings.

Printed in Poland
by Amazon Fulfillment
Poland Sp. z o.o., Wrocław